CHAKRA BOSS:
SLAYING BUSINESS WITH SPIRITUAL SWAG

AUTHOR
KIMBERLY K. WILLIAMS

Table Of Contents

This Book Is Dedicated To:

To the woman who unknowingly crafted the essence of my self-pride and spirituality, my dear mother. Your strength, sass, and unwavering love have shaped me into the force to be reckoned with that I am today, and to all the other women in my life who helped raise me.

To my brother, my eternal business partner and boss motivator, even in his afterlife. Your legacy lives on in every deal closed and every challenge conquered.

To my relentless source of strength and inspiration, my children. You are the fire that fuels my hustle, and the reason I keep pushing boundaries and breaking barriers.

To my dad, the epitome of realness and the truest boss I know. Thank you for teaching me the ropes and instilling in me the grit and determination to conquer whatever comes my way.

To my badass friends, the fierce warriors who keep me grounded and witty with their support and empowerment. You remind me that laughter is the best medicine, especially when served with a side of sass.

To my fellow Bosses who hustle hard, defy odds, and conquer fears through the power of spirituality. Keep shining, keep grinding, and keep manifesting those dreams into reality.

This dedication is a tribute to the powerful souls who have shaped my journey, filled it with purpose, and inspired me to keep slaying with sass and spirit. Here's to us, the unstoppable forces of nature, rewriting the rules and leaving our mark on the world.

With love, wit, and unapologetic sass,

Kim

Introduction:

Uniting Spirituality and Business Success

Lets step into the cutthroat world of business where it's all about bossing up by hustle and making them coins. But honey, there's a new game in town that's mixing ancient spiritual vibes with that modern money grind. Say hello to the world of Chakras!

These spinning energy hubs, straight outta Eastern traditions, are like the superheroes of your soul, each packing a punch with unique powers for your mind, body, and spirit. When these energies are aligned it's like a whole symphony of health, happiness, and vitality to your life. Believe it or not, Chakras have a thing or two to teach us about bossing up too. Picture stability, creativity and confidence - the key ingredients to slay in the business world. By getting in tune with our Chakras, we can tackle work drama like a zen master with the strength of a warrior. Get ready for a wild ride that mixes aligning your chakras with promising business success and personal growth like you never imagined! In "Chakra Boss: Slaying Business With Spiritual Swag ," we're diving deep into each Chakra, linking their vibes to top-tier leadership skills and savvy business moves. Packed with real-life stories, badass exercises, and soul-soothing meditations, get ready to level up your business game through spiritual alignment.

Get set for a life-changing journey that merges your energy with business smarts, making way for a seamless blend of personal and professional success! Trust me, sis, it's gonna be lit!

Chapter 1 : Understanding The Chakras

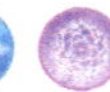

Girl, let me break it down for you real quick. Chakras aren't just some fancy Eastern mumbo jumbo - they're the energy centers in our bodies where all that life force flows through. It's like our energetic GPS, guiding us to physical, emotional, and spiritual harmony.
So, there are seven main Chakras lined up along the spine, from the base right up to the top of the head. Each one has its own vibe, from stability and security at the Root Chakra to love and compassion at the Heart Chakra. And let me tell you, when these Chakras are in sync, life is good. But when one of them is blocked or off balance, Honey, it's like the universe got its wires crossed and now we're dealing with all this chaos in our bodies and minds!

We got the Root Chakra holdin' it down at the base of the spine, keepin' us grounded and stable. Then we got the Sacral Chakra below the navel, all about creativity and emotion - you know, feelin' our feels.
The Solar Plexus Chakra in the belly area! That's where our confidence and personal power come from. And the Heart Chakra? Well, that's all about love and connection. In the throat, we got the Throat Chakra, keepin' our communication game strong. Then the Third Eye Chakra between the eyes - that's where the intuition and vision are at.
Last but not least, the Crown Chakra sittin' pretty at the top of the head, connectin' us to the universe and all that good stuff.

So, buckle up, y'all - we're about to dive deep into each Chakra, see how they can bring some magic to our business and personal lives.

Chapter 2: The Root Chakra In Business - Building a Stable Foundation

Let's talk about the Root Chakra, also known as Muladhara, the OG of the seven Chakras. It's right at the base of your spine. In our bodies, it's all about our basic needs for survival, security, and stability. And guess what? When we're talking biz, these principles are like the secret sauce for building something that lasts.

Keeping It Solid in Business:

Just like the Root Chakra holds down the fort in our personal lives, in business, it's all about nailing down the essentials—like making sure your finances are straight ex: having a business bank account separately from your personal account, your business plan is on point, and your foundation is rock-solid ex: Incorporation, EIN, business address and phone number. When your business is rooted in these things, it can weather any storm and grow like nobody's business.

Why a Strong Foundation Matters:

Listen up, y'all, a business without a solid foundation is like trying to build a mansion on quicksand. You gotta have: Crystal-clear goals and a vision that's tighter than your auntie's Sunday hat. Money matters that are locked down tight and plans for how you're gonna use 'em. A brand that's so trustworthy, folks will give you their last dollar without batting an eye.

Root Chakra Hustle Practices for Business:

If you wanna keep that Root Chakra in check for your biz, here's what you gotta do: Keep a vigilant watch over your finances, like you're hooked on your must-watch series.

Create a workplace vibe that's all about security and stability—no drama, just results. Make decisions based on hard facts and real-deal projections, not just wishful thinking.

Case Study: The Root Chakra in Action - Mama Kim's Bakery

Meet Mama Kim, the proud owner of Mama Kim's Bakery, a small but thriving business known for its mouthwatering treats and warm atmosphere.

Root Chakra Stability: From day one, Mama Kim understood the importance of stability in her business. She made sure to: Secure a prime location for her bakery, ensuring foot traffic and visibility.

Established solid relationships with suppliers, guaranteeing a steady flow of quality ingredients.

Implemented a tight budgeting system, keeping expenses in check and profits steady.

Building a Strong Foundation: Mama Kim knew that a successful business needed a strong foundation. She focused on:

Crafting a clear mission and brand identity, centered around family, tradition, and homemade goodness. Invested in staff training and development, creating a reliable team that shared her passion and values. Prioritizing customer satisfaction, going the extra mile to create memorable experiences and build trust.

Root Chakra Alignment Practices: To keep Mama Kim's Bakery thriving, Mama Kim stayed true to Root Chakra principles by:

Regularly reviewing financial performance and adjusting strategies as needed. Cultivating a welcoming and supportive work environment, where employees felt valued and motivated.

Making strategic decisions based on market trends and customer feedback, ensuring the bakery remained relevant and competitive.

Through Mama Kim's dedication to Root Chakra principles, Mama Kim's Bakery had become a beloved community staple, serving up not just delicious treats, but also a sense of stability and connection for all who walk through its doors.

Alright, sis, let's talk about techniques you can use to strengthen your Root Chakra:

Grounding Meditation:

Find yourself a cozy spot, honey, and settle in. Picture those roots shooting out from your spine or your feet, diving deep into Mama Earth. Feel the strength and steadiness coursing through you with every breath. Focus on feeling rooted and centered, like you're holding down the fort.

Physical Activity:

Get your body moving in ways that connect you with the earth, girl. Kick off your shoes and stroll barefoot on some grass, get your hands dirty in the garden, or strike a pose in yoga —try out Mountain Pose (Tadasana) or TreePose (Vrksasana).

These activities aren't just about getting fit, they're about grounding yourself in the here and now, feeling that stability from head to toe.

Nutrition:

Eat root veggies like carrots, potatoes, beets, you name it. They're like nature's way of saying, "Hey, get grounded!" And don't forget to keep that hydration game strong, 'cause water's the real MVP when it comes to balancing that Root Chakra.

Visualization: Picture a bold, fiery red light right at the base of your spine, representing the Root Chakra power. With each breath you take, watch that red glow get stronger and more fierce, reminding you that you're as secure as they come, and grounded like nobody's business.

Root Chakra Affirmation: Now, repeat after me, loud and proud:
"I'm rooted, stable, and standing on solid ground. I'm as secure as a queen on her throne, connected to Mama Earth in every way. With every breath, I'm building a foundation so strong, nothing's gonna shake me from my personal and professional glow-up!"

Chapter 3: The Sacral Chakra – Get Your Creative Juices Flowing in Business

Alright, bosses, let's talk about your Sacral Chakra, the Svadhishthana. This little gem is all about creativity, passion, and making connections that matter – it's like the social butterfly of your energy centers. When your Sacral Chakra is in check, honey, you're the life of the party and the heart of your business!

Embrace Your Inner Creative Genius:

The Sacral Chakra is where your creative magic happens. Whether you're brainstorming the next big thing or finding innovative solutions, when this chakra is popping, so are your ideas.

Encourage creativity in your workspace. Make it colorful, make it inspiring! Throw some art on the walls, play some good old school r&b – whatever makes your spirit dance.

Relationship Realness:

This chakra isn't just about vibes, it's about deep connections – the kind that make your soul sing. It's all about teamwork, understanding your crew, and vibing with your clients.

Foster an environment in your workplace where folks can speak their truth and understand each other. It's all about respect, communication, and a little bit of fun too!

Adding Spice to Your Sacral Chakra:
Time to let those creative juices flow, darling. Hit up a dance class, put up some paintings, or start a cute project. It's all about expressing yourself and keeping that energy popping.
Relationships are a two-way street, baby. Have regular check-ins with your team, organize team-building activities, or just have a good ol' gossip session over tea. Keep it real and keep it caring.
"The Sacral Sizzle – Let's Fire it Up with an Affirmation: Now, let's amp up those vibes. Place a hand on your belly, right below the navel, feel that energy, and repeat after me:
"I am a fountain of creativity and passion. My connections in business and in life are deep and fulfilling. I embrace my power to create and connect with joy and zest."
Feel that? That's you, turning up the heat in your business and in life.

Chapter 4: The Solar Plexus Chakra – Boss Up and Make Bold Moves

Welcome to the power pad – we're talking about the Solar Plexus Chakra! Situated right above your belly button, this chakra is like the CEO of your energy crew. It's all about personal power, rockin' that self-esteem like your the Queen, and strutting those boss moves. When this chakra is on fire, nobody is gonna rain on your parade in business or life!

Confidence is Your Secret Sauce:

This chakra is where your confidence gets its swag on. It's about owning your flavor, your business, and every choice you make. Doubt? Nah, we don't do that here.

Set the stage for confidence in your workplace. Let your crew know they're valued and their ideas are pure gold. A sprinkle of empowerment goes a long way, honey!

Callin' the Shots Like a Boss:

The Solar Plexus is where the magic of decision-making happens. It's that gut feeling when you know what's what (or what's not) for your business. Trust your gut, but also back it up with some cold, hard facts. It's like having a built-in GPS for your business – it guides you, but you're still the one behind the wheel.

Ignite That Solar Plexus Flame:

Let's turn up the heat in your belly, honey. Pump up those affirmations that boost your self-esteem, dive into new challenges, and don't be afraid to take the lead.

Keep that body movin'' – whether it's kickin' it with martial arts, hitting the pavement for a run, or having a fierce dance-off , get that energy flowin'!

Affirmation Time – Speak Your Power Into Existence:

Stand tall, hand on your belly button, and let's bring the magic:

"I am fierce, capable, and confident. My intuition is sharp, and I make moves with clarity and courage. I lead with strength and grace in my business and beyond."

Feel that vibe? That's your inner boss strutting into the spotlight, ready to slay the day!

Chapter 5: The Heart Chakra – Where Love Meets The Ledger

Welcome to the heart of it all, where the Heart Chakra, aka Anahata, reigns supreme, honey. This is where love, compassion, and connection don't just stroll in but sashay into the office with all the flair and soul you can imagine. When this chakra is singing its tune, it's like your business is giving the world one big, warm hug.

The Rhythm of Business Love:

Picture the Heart Chakra as your emotional savvy sidekick, always nudging you to lead with love and understanding. This isn't just about being nice; it's savvy business, darling.

A business with heart is where people feel seen, clients feel heard, and everybody's part of the tribe. It's about crafting an atmosphere where people don't just clock in; they come alive.

Empathy: Your Superpower Move:

Let's be real, people can sniff out fake kindness like yesterday's leftovers. Genuine empathy – now that's the secret sauce. It's about empathizing with your team's struggles, your client's dreams, and cooking up solutions that truly resonate.

Leading with empathy is like having a magic wand. It helps you vibe with people on a whole other level, build trust, and let's keep it real, it makes you downright lovable.

Heart Chakra TLC – Keeping that Love Alive:

To keep this chakra shining bright, sprinkle a little gratitude and love around. Show your squad some appreciation, pop some champagne for their wins, and let them know they're the real MVPs.

Listening isn't just about hearing; it's about tuning into the heartbeat of others. Hold space for folks to share their stories and feelings. It's like being a soul DJ, spinning the perfect track for the moment.

Affirmation Time – Speak from the Heart:

Place your hand over your heart, feel its rhythm, and let's get those love vibes flowing:

"I lead with love and understanding. My heart guides me to build real connections and nurture relationships rooted in respect and empathy. In my business, every heartbeat contributes to our collective success and harmony."

Let me spin you a real-life tale that brings the Heart Chakra's essence to life:

Meet Barbara, a savvy entrepreneur with a heart of gold and a thriving business in event planning. Barbara's company wasn't just about orchestrating events; it was about creating moments that touched hearts and souls.

One day, Barbara received a call from a client, Staja, who was planning her wedding. Staja was overwhelmed with stress and anxiety, worried that her big day wouldn't live up to her dreams. Barbara could feel the tension in Stajas voice, and her Heart Chakra nudged her to dive deeper.

Instead of just discussing the logistics, Barbara took the time to listen to Stajas hopes and fears, tuning into her emotions. Barbara assured Staja that she wasn't just another client – she was a friend, and Babara was there to make her dreams come true.

With Barbara's empathetic touch, the planning process transformed from a stressful ordeal into a journey filled with love and joy. Barbara went above and beyond, adding personal touches to the wedding that reflected Stajas and her partner's unique love story.

On the big day, as Staja walked down the aisle, tears of joy streamed down her face. Barbara stood in the background, watching the scene unfold with a heart full of gratitude. In that moment, Barbara knew that her business wasn't just about events; it was about weaving love and connection into every detail. Through Barbara's compassionate approach, her business flourished not just because of her expertise but because of the love she poured into every interaction. Barbara's journey was a testament to the power of the Heart Chakra in business – where love truly met the ledger, creating unforgettable moments that touched lives forever.

Feel that warmth? That's the power of love in business, darling.

Chapter 6: The Throat Chakra — Speak Up and Shine in Business

Welcome to the main event, darlings, where we're talking about the Throat Chakra, also known as Vishuddha! This is where your voice, your truth, and your authentic Sass and Wit take center stage. When this chakra is in full swing, your communication is smoother than silk and packs a punch like a diva's hit song.

Unleashing Your Business Voice:

The Throat Chakra is all about letting your voice be heard loud and clear, standing firm by your words like a Boss. It's your inner Beyoncé grabbing that mic in the office, on a call, or during a presentation.

In business, there's no room for mumbling or fumbling. It's about saying what you mean, meaning what you say, and doing it with sass and wit.

The Art of Authentic Expression:

Authenticity isn't just a buzzword, honey, it's your signature move. It's about staying true to your roots and letting your unique flavor shine through in every aspect of your business.

Whether it's in branding, marketing, or everyday convos, let your business's personality sparkle. It's like giving your business its own special sauce – make it unforgettable!

Vocal Vibes – Keeping Your Throat Chakra in Harmony:

Practice communication that's clear as crystal and warm as a summer breeze. It's not just about what you say, it's how you say it. Like a good song, it's the vibe that captures the soul.

Don't hold back, sis. Whether you're pitching a new idea, giving feedback, or standing tall for what you believe in, let your voice ring out loud and proud.

Affirmation Time – Speak It Into Existence:

Gently touch your throat, give it a little clear (ethahhh.... ethahhh) and with all the conviction of a diva, belt out:

"I speak my truth with clarity and confidence. My words carry weight and make waves. In my business, my voice forges real connections and sparks change for the better."

Can you feel that power, honey? That's the magic of a Throat Chakra in perfect harmony, bringing all the sass and shine to your business game.

That's how we keep our Throat Chakra in harmony, making every word we utter in business as impactful as a heartfelt lyric.

Alright, let's talk about the throat chakra and how it's not just about belting out tunes in the shower or dropping wisdom like it's hot—it's a secret weapon in the business game, honey!

Picture this: You're in a high-stakes meeting, trying to seal the deal like the boss you are. Your throat chakra, aka the powerhouse of communication, steps up to the plate. It's not just about talking the talk; it's about speaking your truth with confidence, clarity, and a sprinkle of that signature sass.

When your throat chakra is on point, you're not afraid to pitch that idea, negotiate like a pro, or shut down any nonsense that comes your way. Your words carry weight, your voice commands attention, and you leave no room for doubt or hesitation.

But here's the kicker: it's not just about what you say, but how you say it. Your throat chakra vibes are all about authenticity and integrity. You're not here to play games or put on a show—you're here to speak your truth, loud and proud.

So, whether you're sealing deals, leading meetings, or simply dropping knowledge bombs like confetti, remember to channel that throat chakra energy. Speak up, speak out, and let your voice be heard, because in the world of business, silence isn't golden—it's just missed opportunities, darling!

Chapter 7: The Third Eye Chakra - Visionary Vibes in Business

Welcome to the Third Eye Chakra, or Ajna, where intuition and foresight rule supreme. In the hustle and bustle of business, this chakra drops wisdom and clarity like it's hot. When this chakra is on point, darling, you're not just seeing things as they are, you're seeing the whole cosmic dance.

Intuition: Your Business BFF:

The Third Eye Chakra is all about trusting that inner knowing, that little voice that dishes out genius ideas or gives you the heads up when something's fishy. It's like having your own business whisperer.

In a world where everyone's obsessed with data, never sleep on the power of intuition. It's like having a secret weapon, helping you see beyond the surface and make moves with some serious insight.

A Vision for the Win:

This chakra isn't just about having 20/20 vision; it's about dreaming up your future. It's about setting goals that not only look good on paper but light a fire in your soul.

Keeping Your Third Eye Sharp:

To keep this chakra shining bright, get your mindfulness and meditation game on. It's not just about clearing your mind; it's about opening it wide to the universe's grand buffet of possibilities.

Dive into activities that spark your imagination and get those creative juices flowing. Read books, grab the Boss By Hustle Manifestation, or Gratitude journal, research articles, explore, soak up knowledge like a sponge – feed that Third Eye like it's the VIP at a soulful feast.

Affirmation Time – Visualize and Vocalize:
Close those beauty sleeper (yeah, I know, ironic), gently tap your forehead, and let's declare:
"I trust my gut and ride my vision. My insights steer me towards smart moves that pave the way for my business's long-term greatness. I spot opportunities where others see roadblocks."
Feel that intuition downloading? That's the power of a Third Eye Chakra shining bright in the world of business, baby, and just like that, we've unlocked the visionary potential of the Third Eye Chakra
Alright, picture this: You're strutting into a meeting, feeling like the queen of the hustle that you are, ready to make some serious boss moves. But hold up, sis, before you even open your mouth, let's talk about that third eye chakra and how it's about to take your boss game to a whole new level.
Now, the third eye chakra isn't just some mystical mumbo-jumbo—it's your secret weapon for seeing beyond the surface, tapping into your intuition, and making those savvy business decisions that leave the competition in the dust.
So, here's the scenario: You're faced with a tough call, a make-it-or-break-it decision that could either catapult your business to new heights or send it crashing down like a house of cards. That's where your third eye chakra swoops in like a superhero, giving you that extra dose of intuition and insight to see the bigger picture.
So there I am, sitting in my office, staring at the phone like it's some mystical artifact with the power to shape my destiny. On one end of the line lies the promise of success, like a pot of gold at the end of a rainbow. On the other end? Well, let's just say it's not exactly a walk in the park. But honey, when you're a boss like me, you don't let fear call the shots. Nah, you grab life by the horns and ride it like a bucking bronco at the rodeo.

So I take a deep breath, channeling all the sass and wisdom of my ancestors, and dial that number like I'm punching in the code to the vault of my dreams

With a flick of my perfectly manicured finger, I make the call. The decision that could change everything. And as the words leave my lips, I can practically hear my third eye chuckling in delight, like, "Girl, I told you so."

And wouldn't you know it, the universe answers with a wink and a nod, like it's been waiting for me to make my move all along.
The conversation? Ringggg ringggg.
Voice on the other end: "Well, well, well, look what the cat dragged in. Are you ready to talk business?"
Me: "You bet I am. Let's see what you got."
Voice on the other end: "Oh, I've got something I think you can handle, trust me. Now, let's talk business. I've got an offer you can't refuse."
Me: "Oh, do tell, darling. I'm all ears."
Voice: " I have a position open that I think you would be great for."
Me: "Alright, listen up. I want a seat at the table, and not just any seat. I want the head honcho's chair, with a side of extra perks and a sprinkle of respect."
Voice: "Hmm, bold move, darling. But can you handle the heat?"
Me: "Honey, I eat heat for breakfast and wash it down with a glass of ambition. So what do you say? Are we gonna make magic happen or what?"
Voice: "You drive a hard bargain, but I like your style. Let's make a deal."
Me: "That's what I like to hear. Now, let's shake on it and get this show on the road. I've got places to be and empires to conquer."

And just like that, the deal is done, sealed with a virtual handshake and a promise of greatness on the horizon.

You're not just relying on facts and figures—you're tapping into your gut instincts, your inner wisdom, and those divine downloads from the universe. Whether it's sniffing out a shady deal, spotting a golden opportunity, or navigating through the twists and turns of the business world, your third eye chakra is your ultimate hustle buddy.

But here's the kicker: you gotta trust it, sis. Trust that inner voice, trust those gut feelings, and trust that you're always being guided towards your highest good. Because when you align your hustle with your intuition, there ain't no mountain high enough, no deal too tricky, and no obstacle you can't overcome.

So, boss up, tune in, and let that third eye chakra lead the way. Because in the game of hustle, it's not just about making moves—it's about making magic happen, one intuitive decision at a time.

Chapter 8: The Crown Chakra - Elevating Business to a Higher Plane

Welcome to the grand finale of our chakra journey, we're talking about the Crown Chakra, aka Sahasrara. Positioned right at the tippy-top of your head, this chakra is your spiritual hotline to something bigger than yourself – whether it's the universe, a higher power, or your own divine essence. When it's shining bright, baby, your business isn't just a business; it's a divine calling.

The Spiritual Symphony of Success:

The Crown Chakra is about realizing that your business is just one note in the grand symphony of life. It's about finding purpose beyond profit, recognizing your ripple effect on the world, and dancing to the rhythm of your true essence. Imagine your business as a sacred dance, a collaboration with the universe that moves hearts, minds, and souls. It's about intertwining your purpose into every fiber of your being and business.

Soulful Business Vibes:

This chakra invites you to ponder the profound questions: Why does my business exist? Who am I serving? What legacy am I creating?

A soul-driven business resonates on a deeper frequency with your team, attracting people who vibe with your vision and mission. It's not just about what you do; it's about why you do it – the soul fuel that ignites your journey.

Crowning Glory – Nurturing Your Divine Connection:
To keep this chakra shining like a beacon in the night, indulge in practices that elevate your energy. Dive into meditation, pour your soul into reflective writing, grab the Boss By Hustle Bundle Pack that includes the Gratitude Journal, Manifestation Journal and the Affirmation Planner and bask in the beauty of nature's embrace.
Take time to revisit and reflect on your business's mission and vision. Ensure they dance in harmony with your deepest values and contribute to the symphony of global transformation.
Affirmation Time – Reach for the Stars:
Place your hand gently on top of your crown, and with the power of purpose, declare:
"I am a vessel for divine purpose through my business. I lead with spiritual vision and unwavering integrity, birthing positive transformation. My work is an ode to my highest self, a melody of love echoing through eternity." Feel that connection pulsating through your being? That, my dear, is your Crown Chakra aligning your business with the universe!
Honey, with the Crown Chakra, we've hit the mountaintop of our chakra and business odyssey, mixing spirituality with strategy for a business journey that's downright divine. Now, with all our chakras lined up like they're ready to strut the catwalk, you're geared up to tackle the business world with a cocktail of wisdom and creativity all aligned.
Alright, honey, let's spice up that crown chakra with some soulful and sassy eats! Here's how to align your vibe and elevate your hustle: Sip on Some Tea: Ain't nothing like starting your day with a cup of herbal tea that's brewed with love and wisdom. Get your hands on some chamomile or peppermint tea, and let those flavors dance on your palate like it's your own personal party.

Green Goddess Goodness: Get your greens on, honey! Whip up a mean salad loaded with kale, spinach, and all the leafy goodness your crown chakra desires. Top it off with some avocado slices and sprinkle it with seeds for that extra crunch.

Fruit Fiesta: Dive into a bowl of fresh, juicy berries like it's a celebration of life itself. Blueberries, strawberries, raspberries—you name it, babe! These little bursts of sweetness will not only satisfy your cravings but also give your crown chakra the boost it needs to shine bright like a diamond.

Spice Up Your Life: Don't be afraid to get spicy, darling! Add a pinch of turmeric, a dash of ginger, or a sprinkle of cinnamon to your meals and watch as your taste buds do a happy dance. These spices isn't just for flavor—they're like magic that awaken your senses and ignite your spirit.

Chocolate Dreams: Treat yourself to a little indulgence with some dark chocolate goodness. Not only does it satisfy your sweet tooth, but it also gives your brain a little love with its antioxidant-rich goodness. So go ahead, indulge in a square or two (or three)—you deserve it!

Mindful Munching: Slow down, baby, and savor each and every bite like it's a divine experience. Eating mindfully isn't just about nourishing your body—it's about feeding your soul and connecting with the energy of your food. So chew slowly, chew sassily, and let those flavors transport you to a higher plane of existence.With these soulful and sassy eats, you'll have your crown chakra beaming brighter than a disco ball at midnight, ready to conquer the world with style, grace, and a whole lot of bossy sass.

Bonus Section:

Kickin' Anxiety to the Curb - In Life and Business

Alright, loves, let's chat about showing anxiety the door in both our personal and professional worlds. Anxiety? Honey, it's like that party crasher who's overstayed their welcome. But fear not, we're about to give it the boot.

1. Inhale the Good Stuff :

When anxiety comes knocking, take a deep breath, and I mean deep. Inhale the good vibes, exhale the drama. It's like giving your soul a pep talk. Dive into some breathing exercises or a quick meditation sesh. Picture each breath as a wave washing away those pesky worries.

2. Shake it Off with a Dance Break:

Crank up those old school hits and let loose with a dance party, right where you are. Dancing isn't just fun; it's a one-way ticket to Stress-Freeville, Anxiety, who?

3. Mindset Makeover:

In business, flip the script on those anxious thoughts. Instead of "What if I mess up?" try "What can I learn?" Shift from fear to curiosity – it's a game-changer.

Grab your Boss By Hustle journal or have a 'win' list handy to remind yourself of all the boss moves you've made. It's like your personal hype squad.

4. Squad Goals:

Surround yourself with positive vibes only – your ride-or-die crew. Whether it's your tribe, fam, or work squad, their energy can turn your day around.

In business, create a team vibe that's all about lifting each other up. It's about having each other's backs, no matter what.

5. Treat Yourself: Pamper yourself with some self-care. Whether it's a spa day, diving into a good book, or just some quiet time, recharge those batteries, honey. Remember, your mental health matters in life and in business. If anxiety's cranking up the volume, talking to a pro is the ultimate power move.

Affirmation for Anxiety-Free Living:

Let's seal this with an affirmation fit for Boss Ladies Everywhere . Hand on heart, repeat after me:

"I am more powerful than my anxiety. In life and in business, I choose bravery over worry, action over fear. Every step I take is a strut towards peace and success."

Conclusion: Strutting into Success – A Chakra-Inspired Business Journey

Honey, we've danced through the chakras, from the grounding vibes of the Root to the lofty realms of the Crown, and what a journey it's been! Each chakra, with its unique energy and lessons, has shown us how to infuse our businesses with soul, swag, and a whole lot of smarts.
The Full Spectrum of Success:
Remember, my fabulous Bosses, business success isn't just about the numbers; it's about the energy you bring to every deal, every plan, and every day. These chakras aren't just spiritual concepts; they're practical tools to keep you balanced, inspired, and aligned.
From the Root to the Crown, each chakra has offered us wisdom on stability, creativity, confidence, love, communication, insight, and purpose. When harmonized, they turn you not just into a business owner, but a business force.
Beyond the Office: This isn't just about thriving in the market; it's about thriving in life. When your chakras are aligned, you're not just a better boss; you're a better you. You're living proof that when you bring your whole, authentic self to your work, magic happens. And let's not forget, this journey is also about the vibe you put out into the
world. Your business can be a beacon of positivity, a catalyst for change, and a testament to your personal journey.

Keep Shining, Keep Bossing Up By Hustle:
As we close this book, remember that the journey with your chakras is ongoing. They're like old friends who have your back – check in with them, nurture them, and let them guide you.
Whether you're negotiating a deal, brainstorming your next big project, or just sitting down with a cup of coffee to plan your day, remember: You have the power, the wisdom, and the soul to make it extraordinary. So, strut into your business world with confidence, darling. Keep that head high, heart open, and spirit bright. You've got a whole chakra squad behind you, and girl, you're going to make it spectacular!

SEVEN CHAKRAS

CROWN
Sahajrara

THIRD EYE
Ajna

THROAT
Vishuddha

HEART
Anahata

SOLAR PLEXUS
Manipura

SACRAL
Svadhisthana

ROOT
Muladhata

The crown (7th chakra) is located at the top of the head. It represents states of higher consciousnessand divine connettion. Imbalanced attributes would be cynicism, disregarding what is sacred, closed mindedness, and disconnection with spirit.

The third eye (6th chakra) is located in the center of the forehead, between the eyebrows. It represents intuitioni foresight, and is driven by openness and imagination. Imbalanced attributes would be lack of direction and lack of clarity.

The throat (5th chakra) is located at the center of the neck. It represents the ability to speak and communicate clearly and effectively. Imbalanced attributes would be shyness, being withdrawn, arrogance and increased anxiety.

The heart (4th chakra) is located in the center of the chest. It represents love, self-love, and governs our relationships. Imbalanced attributes would be depression, difficulty in relationships, and lack of self-discipline.

The solar plexus (3rd chakra) is located below the chest. It represents self-esteem, pleasure, will-power, and personal responsibility. Imbalanced attribustes would be low self-esteem, control issues, manipulative tendencies, and minuse of power.

The sacral (2nd chakra) is located below the navel. It represents creative and sexual energies. Imbalanced attributes would be lack of or repressed creativity, sexual dysfunction, withheld intimacy, and emotional isolation.

The root (1st chakra) is located at the base of the spine. It provides the foundation on which we build our life, representing safety, security, and stability. Imbalanced attributes would be scattered energies, anxiety, and fear.